April Fools' Day
to
Z Day

Holidays from A to Z

Colleen Dolphin

Consulting Editor, Diane Craig, M.A./Reading Specialist

ABDO
Publishing Company

Published by ABDO Publishing Company, 8000 West 78th Street, Edina, Minnesota 55439. Copyright © 2009 by Abdo Consulting Group, Inc. International copyrights reserved in all countries. No part of this book may be reproduced in any form without written permission from the publisher. Super SandCastle™ is a trademark and logo of ABDO Publishing Company.

Printed in the United States.

Editor: Martha E. H. Rustad
Content Developer: Nancy Tuminelly
Cover and Interior Design and Production: Colleen Dolphin, Mighty Media
Photo Credits: Brand X Pictures, iStockphoto/Jani Bryson, Shutterstock

Library of Congress Cataloging-in-Publication Data

Dolphin, Colleen, 1979-
  April Fools' Day to Z Day : holidays from A to Z / Colleen Dolphin.
    p. cm. -- (Let's learn A to Z)
  ISBN 978-1-60453-495-5
  1. Holidays--United States--Juvenile literature. 2. Holidays--Juvenile literature. 3. English language--Alphabet--Juvenile literature. 4. Alphabet books--Juvenile literature. I. Title.

GT4803.D58 2009
394.26973--dc22
                          2008023992

Super SandCastle™ books are created by a team of professional educators, reading specialists, and content developers around five essential components— phonemic awareness, phonics, vocabulary, text comprehension, and fluency— to assist young readers as they develop reading skills and strategies and increase their general knowledge. All books are written, reviewed, and leveled for guided reading, early reading intervention, and Accelerated Reader® programs for use in shared, guided, and independent reading and writing activities to support a balanced approach to literacy instruction.

About Super SandCastle™

Bigger Books for Emerging Readers
Grades K–4

Created for library, classroom, and at-home use, Super SandCastle™ books support and engage young readers as they develop and build literacy skills and will increase their general knowledge about the world around them. Super SandCastle™ books are part of SandCastle™, the leading preK–3 imprint for emerging and beginning readers. Super SandCastle™ features a larger trim size for more reading fun.

Let Us Know

Super SandCastle™ would like to hear your stories about reading this book. What was your favorite page? Was there something hard that you needed help with? Share the ups and downs of learning to read. We want to hear from you! Send us an e-mail.

sandcastle@abdopublishing.com

Contact us for a complete list of SandCastle™, Super SandCastle™, and other nonfiction and fiction titles from ABDO Publishing Company.

www.abdopublishing.com • 8000 West 78th Street Edina, MN 55439 • 800-800-1312 • 952-831-1632 fax

This fun and informative series employs illustrated definitions to introduce emerging readers to an alphabet of words in various topic areas. Each page combines words with corresponding images and descriptive sentences to encourage learning and knowledge retention. AlphagalorZ inspires young readers to find out more about the subjects that most interest them!

The "Guess what?" feature expands the reading and learning experience by offering additional information and fascinating facts about specific words or concepts. The "More Words" section provides additional related A to Z vocabulary words that develop and increase reading comprehension.

These books are appropriate for library, classroom, and home use.

Aa

Guess what?

Sometimes there are fake stories in the newspaper on April Fools' Day.

April Fools' Day

April Fools' Day is celebrated on April 1st. It is a day to play harmless jokes on your friends and family. If the person believes the joke, that person is fooled!

Birthday

Birthdays are celebrated once a year on the date a person was born. It is a tradition to have a cake with candles on top. The birthday person makes a wish before blowing out the candles.

Bb

5

Christmas

Christmas is a Christian holiday. It celebrates the birth of Jesus. Christmas is on December 25th. As a custom, many people decorate a tree inside their home. They place gifts under the tree for one another.

Cc

Day of the Dead

Day of the Dead is a Christian holiday that is celebrated mostly in Mexico. It is on November 2nd. Day of the Dead is a time to remember people who have died. It is common to visit and decorate graves where loved ones are buried.

7

Dd

Earth Day

Earth Day was started by a Wisconsin senator in 1970. It is celebrated around April 22nd. There are parades and other events on Earth Day. They remind people to stop polluting and help save the earth.

Ee

Father's Day

Father's Day is celebrated in many parts of the world. In the United States, Father's Day is on the third Sunday of June. Fathers, and sometimes grandfathers or uncles, are honored on this day.

Guess what?

The first Father's Day was celebrated in 1910, but it wasn't an official holiday until 1966.

Gg

Guess what?

The same groundhog in Pennsylvania is watched each year. His name is Punxsutawney Phil.

Groundhog Day

Groundhog Day is celebrated in the United States and Canada on February 2nd. It is believed that a groundhog can forecast the weather on this day. If the groundhog sees its shadow there will be six more weeks of winter. If not, the weather will be mild for the next six weeks.

Hanukkah

Hanukkah is a Jewish holiday. It lasts for eight days during December. Jews celebrate part of their history during this time. They light a candle each day.

Hh

Ii

Independence Day

Independence Day is observed on July 4th in the United States. It celebrates the U.S. separation from Great Britain. It is a tradition to have parades and watch fireworks on this holiday.

Juneteenth

Juneteenth is a U.S. holiday that observes the end of slavery. It is on June 19th. Juneteenth is a time to celebrate freedom and learn about history.

Guess what?

Ralph Ellison was a famous African American writer. He wrote a book called *Juneteenth*.

Kwanzaa

Kwanzaa is an African American holiday celebrated from December 26th to January 1st. It honors African American families and cultures. People honor a different principle on each day of Kwanzaa.

Guess what?

On December 31st, families have a feast called *karamu*.

Kk

14

Labor Day

Labor Day is on the first Monday in September in the United States and Canada. On this day, workers are recognized for what they do for their communities.

15

Mother's Day

Mother's Day is celebrated in the United States and many other parts of the world. In the United States, Mother's Day is on the second Sunday in May. Mothers, and sometimes grandmothers and aunts, are honored on Mother's Day.

Guess what?

Mother's Day became a U.S. national holiday in 1914.

Mm

New Year's Day

New Year's Day celebrates the beginning of a new year. January 1st is New Year's Day in the United States. It is on a different day in some cultures.

Guess what?

One tradition is to make a promise at the start of a new year. This is called a New Year's resolution.

Nn

Oo

Guess what?

Many people celebrate Opposite Day on January 24th.

Opposite Day

Opposite Day can be celebrated at any time. On opposite day everything people say or do is different from what they mean. If a person says "I'm sad," that person is actually happy!

Passover

Passover is a Jewish holiday during March or April. It celebrates their freedom from slavery hundreds of years ago. Passover lasts for seven to eight days.

Guess what?

On the first night of Passover families have a dinner called the seder. Each item they eat symbolizes how the Jewish people became free.

Qq

Women's EQuality Day

Women's Equality Day is a U.S. holiday. It is on August 26th. It was started in 1970. It celebrates equality between women and men.

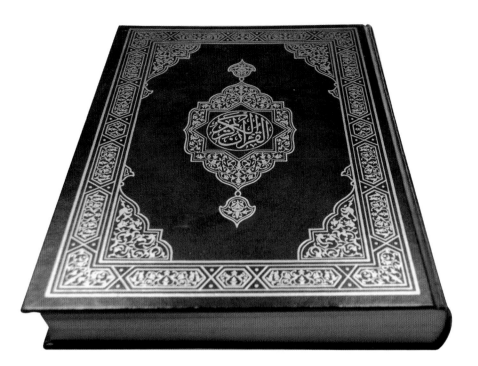

Ramadan

Ramadan is an Islamic holiday. It lasts for one month. It celebrates the gift of the Qur'an. The Qur'an is a book that guides Muslims.

Rr

Saint Patrick's Day

Saint Patrick's Day is a Christian holiday observed on March 17th. It celebrates the life of Saint Patrick. He built many churches and schools in Ireland about 1,600 years ago.

Guess what?

An Irish legend says Saint Patrick scared all of the snakes out of Ireland.

Ss

22

Thanksgiving

Thanksgiving is a holiday in the United States and Canada. Thanksgiving is a time to give thanks. The feast shared by the Pilgrims and the Native Americans in 1621 was the first Thanksgiving.

Guess what?

In the United States, Thanksgiving is the fourth Thursday in November. In Canada, it is the second Monday in October.

23

Uu

United Nations Day

United Nations Day is observed on October 24th. The United Nations is a group of about 200 countries. Their purpose is to build world peace. On United Nations Day, all of the countries celebrate the hope for peace.

Valentine's Day

Valentine's Day is celebrated in many countries. It is on February 14th. It is a day to show love and friendship. It is a custom to give cards and candy on Valentine's Day.

Be Mine

Guess what?

A heart is a symbol of Valentine's Day.

Vv

25

Ww

World Kindness Day

World Kindness Day is on November 13th. It is a day for the whole world to celebrate peace. Although there are many different cultures, everyone is equal.

Guess what?

RelaXation Day is sometimes observed on August 15th.

RelaXation Day

Relaxation Day can be celebrated by anyone on any day. It is a day to do nothing. Taking a day to relax is good for a person's health.

Yom Kippur

Yom Kippur is a Jewish holiday. It is in September or October. It is a serious time when Jewish people ask God and others for forgiveness, and try to forgive others.

Yy

28

Guess what?

Jewish people spend the day of Yom Kippur praying. When they are done, they blow a horn called the *shofar*.

Z Day

Z Day can be observed at any time. It is a day when things are alphabetized from Z to A. Names and things that start with A usually get to go first. On Z Day, names and things that start with Z get to go first for a change!

Glossary

celebrate – to honor with special ceremonies or festivities.

Christian – having to do with the religion Christianity.

culture – the behavior, beliefs, art, and other products of a particular group of people.

custom – a tradition practiced by people in a particular region or area.

decorate – to make something or someplace look festive or pretty.

forecast – to say what is likely to happen in the future based on facts and information.

grave – a place where a dead person or animal is buried.

Islam – a religion that follows the teachings of Muhammad. People who follow Islam are called Muslims.

Jesus – the founder of Christianity. Christians believe he was the son of god.

Jewish – having to do with the religion Judaism.

legend – a story passed down through history that may not be true.

national – having to do with a whole nation.

Pilgrims – a group of people who came from England to America in the 1600s.

pollute – to contaminate air, water, or soil with man-made waste.

principle – a rule or belief.

resolution – a decision to do something.

senator – in government, a person elected to the senate, a group of people that makes laws at the state or national level.

serious – solemn or thoughtful.

shadow – the darker area created when something blocks the light of the sun or another light source.

slavery – the practice of owning and controlling people.

symbol – an object that represents something else.

symbolize – to represent something else with an object.

tradition – customs, practices, or beliefs passed from one generation to the next.

More Holidays!

Can you learn about these holidays too?

Advent	Easter	National Quilting Day
All Saints' Day	Election Day	Palm Sunday
Arbor Day	Epiphany	Parents' Day
Armed Forces Day	Flag Day	Patriot Day
Ash Wednesday	Good Friday	Pearl Harbor Day
Bastille Day	Grandparents' Day	Presidents' Day
Boss's Day	Halloween	Rosh Hashanah
Chinese New Year	Leap Day	St. Nicholas Day
Cinco de Mayo	Mardi Gras	Solstice
Columbus Day	Martin Luther King Jr. Day	Veterans Day
Cousins' Day	May Day	Washington's Birthday
Diwali	Memorial Day	World AIDS Day